NEW View

Rain FOREST

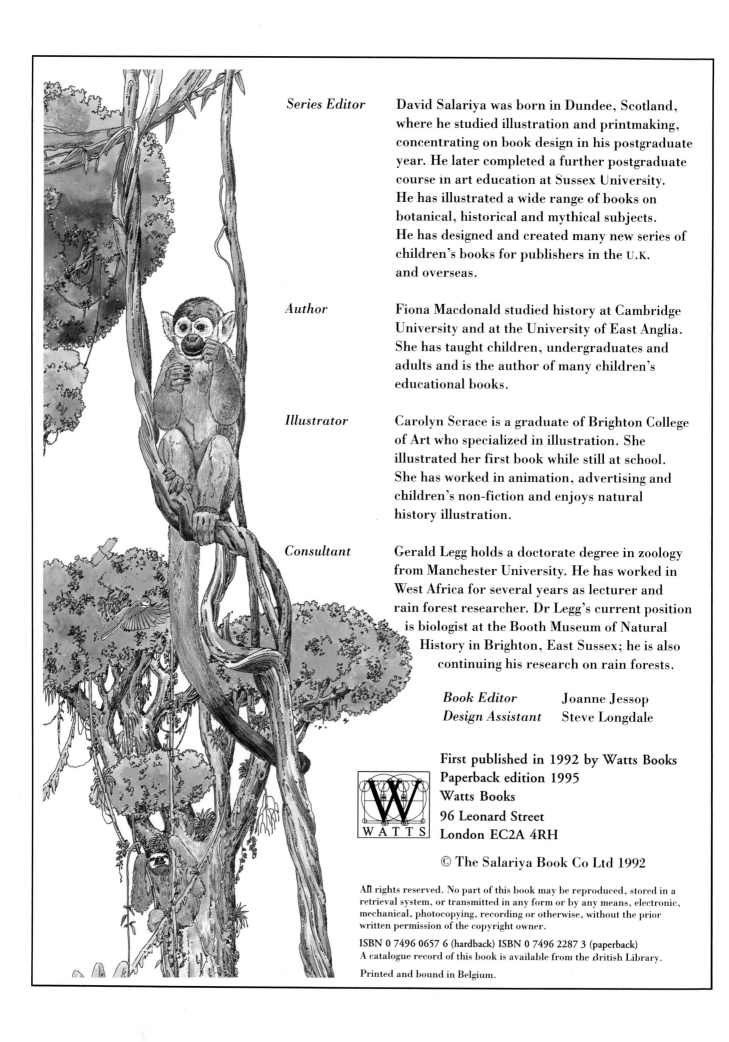

Series Editor — David Salariya was born in Dundee, Scotland, where he studied illustration and printmaking, concentrating on book design in his postgraduate year. He later completed a further postgraduate course in art education at Sussex University. He has illustrated a wide range of books on botanical, historical and mythical subjects. He has designed and created many new series of children's books for publishers in the U.K. and overseas.

Author — Fiona Macdonald studied history at Cambridge University and at the University of East Anglia. She has taught children, undergraduates and adults and is the author of many children's educational books.

Illustrator — Carolyn Scrace is a graduate of Brighton College of Art who specialized in illustration. She illustrated her first book while still at school. She has worked in animation, advertising and children's non-fiction and enjoys natural history illustration.

Consultant — Gerald Legg holds a doctorate degree in zoology from Manchester University. He has worked in West Africa for several years as lecturer and rain forest researcher. Dr Legg's current position is biologist at the Booth Museum of Natural History in Brighton, East Sussex; he is also continuing his research on rain forests.

Book Editor — Joanne Jessop
Design Assistant — Steve Longdale

First published in 1992 by Watts Books
Paperback edition 1995
Watts Books
96 Leonard Street
London EC2A 4RH

© The Salariya Book Co Ltd 1992

ISBN 0 7496 0657 6 (hardback) ISBN 0 7496 2287 3 (paperback)
A catalogue record of this book is available from the British Library.

Printed and bound in Belgium.

NEW View · Rain FOREST

Written by
FIONA MACDONALD

Illustrated by
CAROLYN SCRACE

Created & Designed by
DAVID SALARIYA

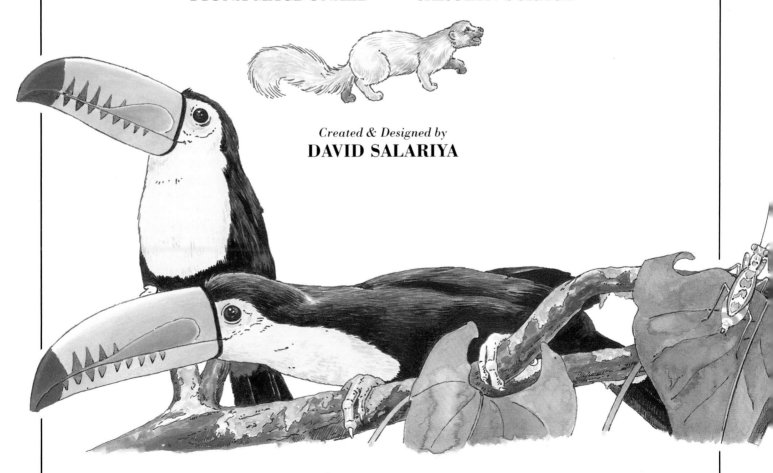

WATTS BOOK
London • New York • Sydney

Contents

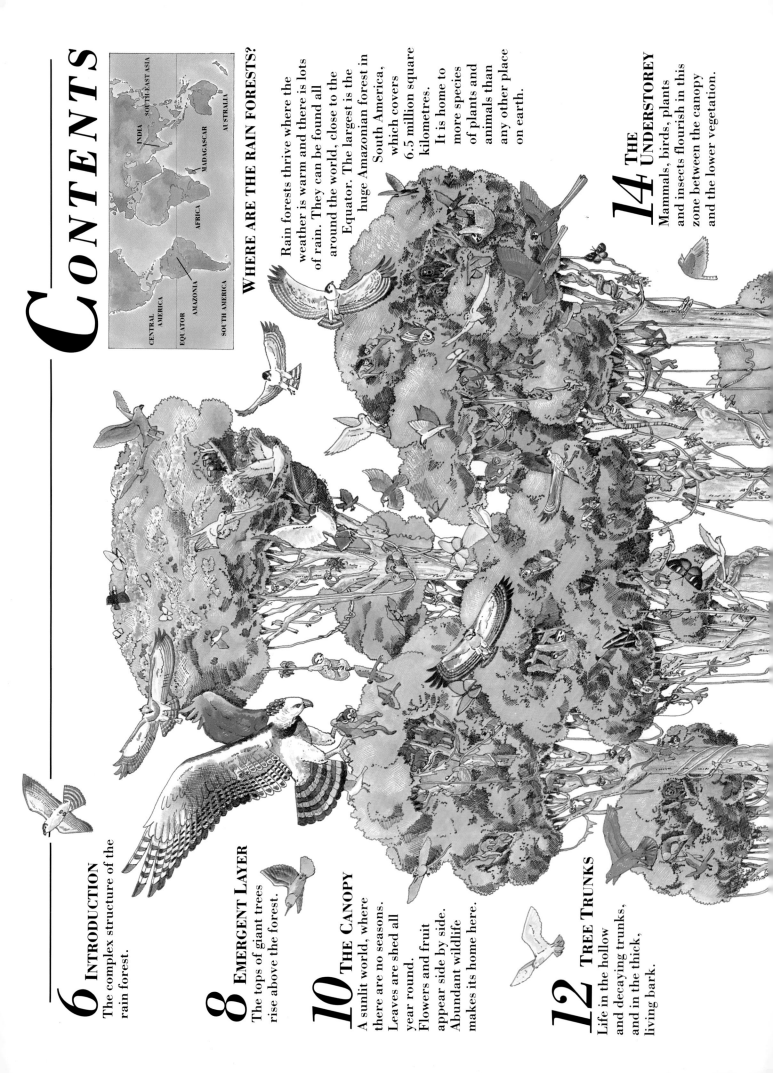

6 INTRODUCTION
The complex structure of the rain forest.

8 EMERGENT LAYER
The tops of giant trees rise above the forest.

10 THE CANOPY
A sunlit world, where there are no seasons. Leaves are shed all year round. Flowers and fruit appear side by side. Abundant wildlife makes its home here.

12 TREE TRUNKS
Life in the hollow and decaying trunks, and in the thick, living bark.

14 THE UNDERSTOREY
Mammals, birds, plants and insects flourish in this zone between the canopy and the lower vegetation.

WHERE ARE THE RAIN FORESTS?

Rain forests thrive where the weather is warm and there is lots of rain. They can be found all around the world, close to the Equator. The largest is the huge Amazonian forest in South America, which covers 6.5 million square kilometres. It is home to more species of plants and animals than any other place on earth.

INDIA
SOUTH-EAST ASIA
AUSTRALIA
MADAGASCAR
AFRICA
CENTRAL AMERICA
EQUATOR
AMAZONIA
SOUTH AMERICA

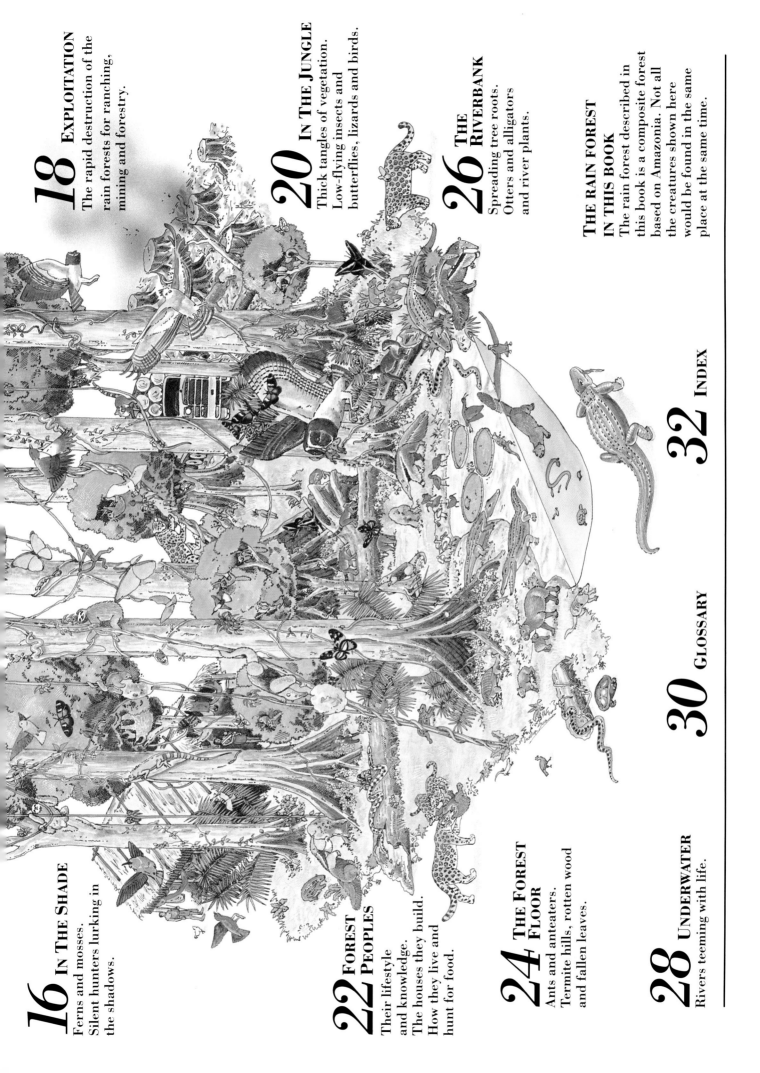

16 IN THE SHADE
Ferns and mosses.
Silent hunters lurking in
the shadows.

18 EXPLOITATION
The rapid destruction of the
rain forests for ranching,
mining and forestry.

20 IN THE JUNGLE
Thick tangles of vegetation.
Low-flying insects and
butterflies, lizards and birds.

22 FOREST PEOPLES
Their lifestyle
and knowledge.
The houses they build.
How they live and
hunt for food.

24 THE FOREST FLOOR
Ants and anteaters.
Termite hills, rotten wood
and fallen leaves.

26 THE RIVERBANK
Spreading tree roots.
Otters and alligators
and river plants.

28 UNDERWATER
Rivers teeming with life.

30 GLOSSARY

32 INDEX

THE RAIN FOREST IN THIS BOOK
The rain forest described in
this book is a composite forest
based on Amazonia. Not all
the creatures shown here
would be found in the same
place at the same time.

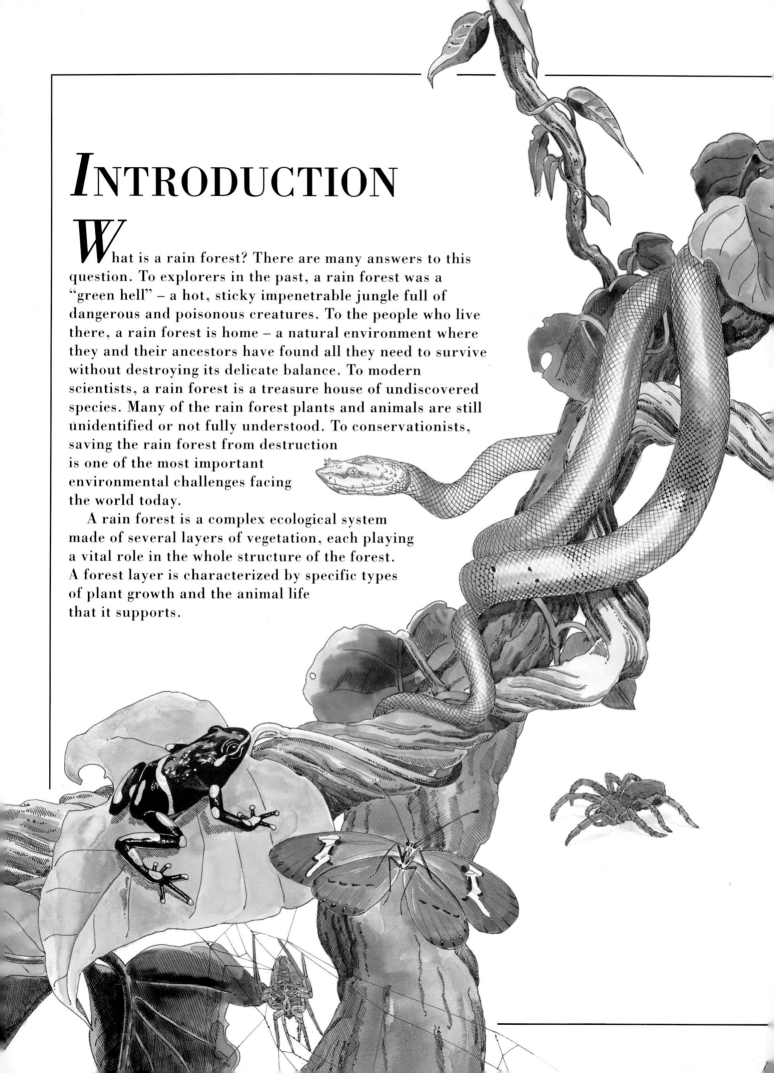

INTRODUCTION

What is a rain forest? There are many answers to this question. To explorers in the past, a rain forest was a "green hell" – a hot, sticky impenetrable jungle full of dangerous and poisonous creatures. To the people who live there, a rain forest is home – a natural environment where they and their ancestors have found all they need to survive without destroying its delicate balance. To modern scientists, a rain forest is a treasure house of undiscovered species. Many of the rain forest plants and animals are still unidentified or not fully understood. To conservationists, saving the rain forest from destruction is one of the most important environmental challenges facing the world today.

A rain forest is a complex ecological system made of several layers of vegetation, each playing a vital role in the whole structure of the forest. A forest layer is characterized by specific types of plant growth and the animal life that it supports.

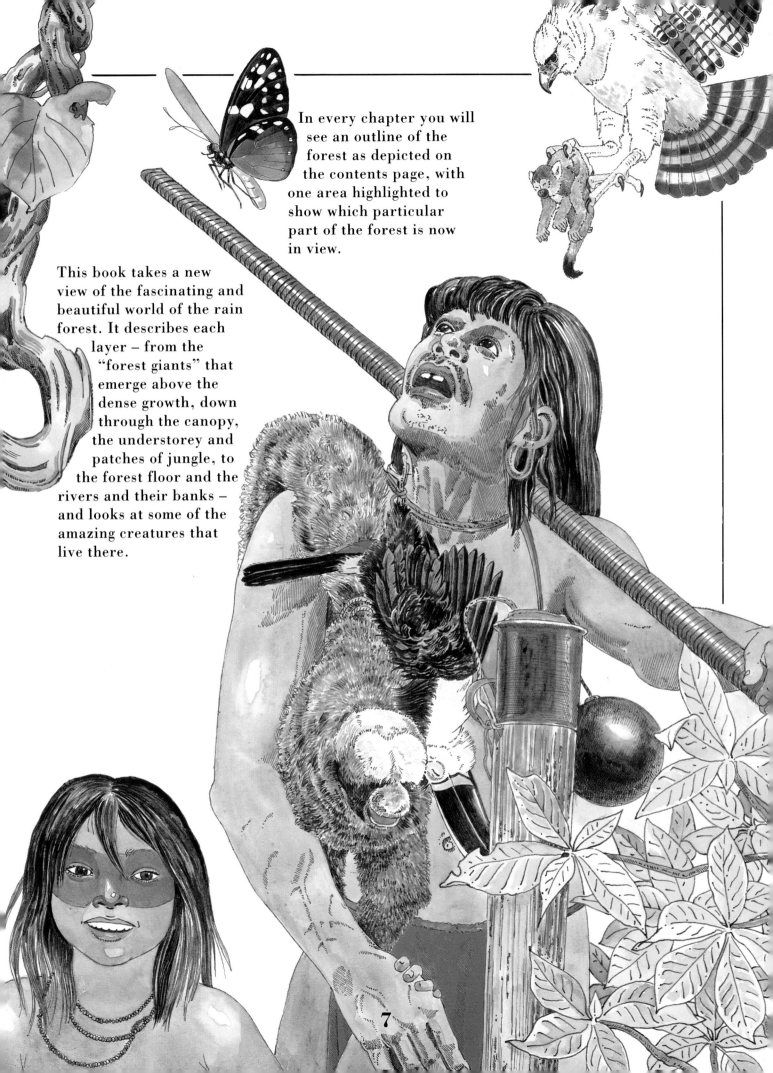

In every chapter you will see an outline of the forest as depicted on the contents page, with one area highlighted to show which particular part of the forest is now in view.

This book takes a new view of the fascinating and beautiful world of the rain forest. It describes each layer – from the "forest giants" that emerge above the dense growth, down through the canopy, the understorey and patches of jungle, to the forest floor and the rivers and their banks – and looks at some of the amazing creatures that live there.

7

• Vultures soar high above the trees, drifting on currents of warm air rising from the forest. Their keen eyesight helps them spot prey far below.

• Because they have plenty of space in which to grow, the trees of the emergent layer develop wide, bushy crowns shaped like umbrellas.

• The tallest trees have long, pointed leaves that allow heavy rainfall to run off. If the leaves stayed wet, they would soon rot.

• One fifth of the world's bird population lives in the tall trees of the Amazonian forest.

• Seeds from the "forest giants" are carried by the wind. They travel vast distances high above the forest before they eventually fall to the ground.

EMERGENT LAYER

The tallest trees in the rain forest emerge majestically above the thick canopy of branches and leaves to reach the sunlight. There are only one or two of these "forest giants" per hectare of forest. Their giant height – over 40 metres – gives them advantages: more light and more space to grow. When they eventually fall, weakened by age, root damage or disease, their massive trunks create a wide clearing as they smash through the undergrowth.

Although they are very tall, the great forest trees have shallow roots. To support their weight, many species have developed buttress roots, spreading outwards from the trunk and reaching down to the forest floor.

KEY

1. Jackamar
2. King vultures
3. Erythrina tree with communal weaver bird nests
4. Bromeliad flowers
5. Quetzal
6. Pygmy anteater
7. Crown of "forest giant"
8. Mist rising above canopy
9. Green-winged macaw
10. Dusky jacobin
11. Green-cheeked Amazon hummingbird
12. Branches and leaves forming a canopy
13. Morpho butterfly
14. Toucans
15. Black-headed squirrel monkey
16. Hyacinth macaw
17. Male topaz hummingbird
18. Bromeliad
19. Female topaz hummingbird
20. Spider monkey
21. Amazilia dumerilii hummingbird

• The rain forest receives over 6000 millimetres of rainfall each year. But the canopy stops 80 per cent of this moisture from ever reaching the ground.

• The canopy blocks out about 98 per cent of the sunlight.

• Because canopy trees are crowded for space, they have knobbly, club-shaped crowns.

THE CANOPY

*T*he branches and leaves that grow at the tops of tall, slender trunks form a thick layer of vegetation known as the canopy. This main layer of the rain forest is between 30 and 40 metres above the ground. Some canopy trees produce enormous leaves, up to 6 metres long.

The majority of rain forest animals make their homes in the canopy, where the thick vegetation provides shelter and plenty to eat. Colourful birds dart among the leaves. Monkeys swing from branch to branch in search of food. Mammals that live in the canopy are skilful climbers and rarely descend to the forest floor. The sloth, for example, comes down from the trees about once a month when it uses the forest floor as a toilet.

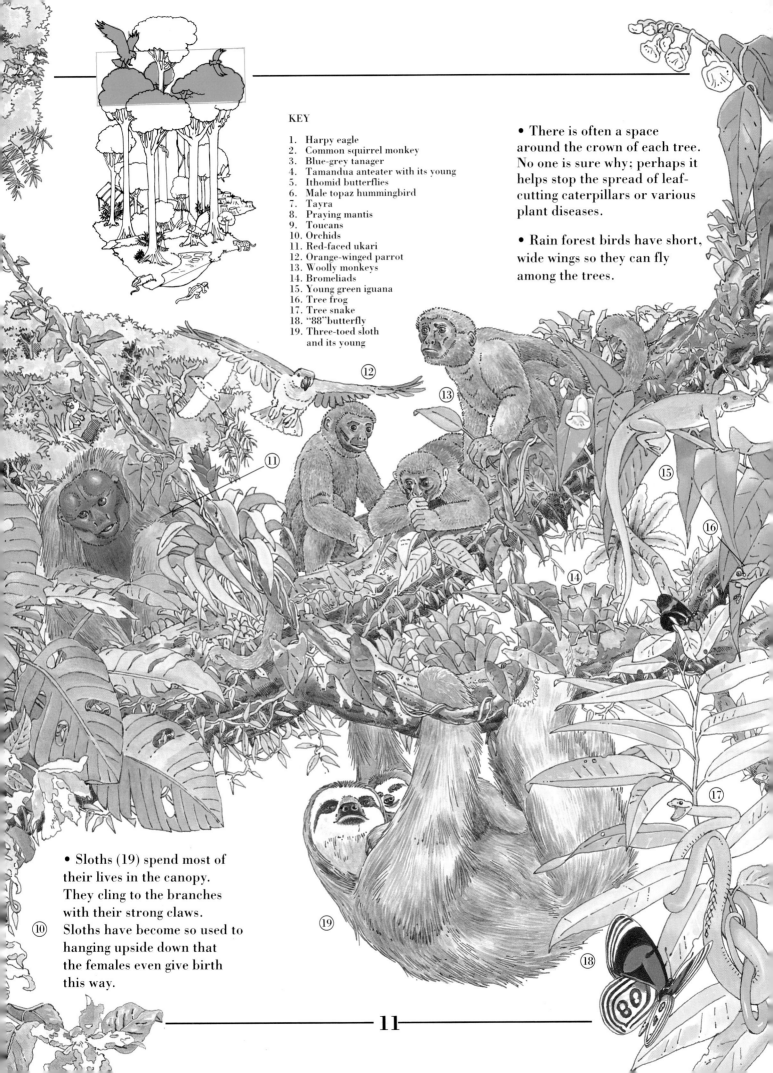

KEY

1. Harpy eagle
2. Common squirrel monkey
3. Blue-grey tanager
4. Tamandua anteater with its young
5. Ithomid butterflies
6. Male topaz hummingbird
7. Tayra
8. Praying mantis
9. Toucans
10. Orchids
11. Red-faced ukari
12. Orange-winged parrot
13. Woolly monkeys
14. Bromeliads
15. Young green iguana
16. Tree frog
17. Tree snake
18. "88" butterfly
19. Three-toed sloth and its young

• There is often a space around the crown of each tree. No one is sure why; perhaps it helps stop the spread of leaf-cutting caterpillars or various plant diseases.

• Rain forest birds have short, wide wings so they can fly among the trees.

• Sloths (19) spend most of their lives in the canopy. They cling to the branches with their strong claws. Sloths have become so used to hanging upside down that the females even give birth this way.

TREE TRUNKS

High above the forest floor
fertile gardens of orchids,
mosses and ferns grow on the tree trunks. Soil in the crevices of
tree trunks provides homes for creatures such as worms that
are normally found on the ground. Water collects in the bark or
in cup-shaped bromeliad plants to form drinking pools and
even small ponds where frogs can lay their eggs.

Lizards, snakes, bats, frogs, moths, butterflies and small
mammals all make their homes in the tree trunks. Some tree
creatures spend their whole lives here and never reach the
forest floor. Others, such as wasps and ants, travel up and
down, using raw materials from the trees for nests or for food.
Some are camouflaged, to help them catch their prey, while
others are brightly coloured, to protect them from attack.

• Leaf-cutter ants (8) chew off
fragments of leaves and carry
them to their underground
nests. There, the ants mix the
leaves with fungus spores,
which germinate on the
decaying leaves. When the
fungus is fully grown, the ants
use it to feed their young.

• Paper wasps (7) build
beautiful, fragile nests,
as fine as paper, out of chewed
wood-pulp.

KEY
1. Katydid
2. Pike-headed vine snake
3. Forest iguana
4. Epiphytes
5. Ferns
6. Mosses
7. Paper wasp
8. Leaf-cutter ants
9. Flowering epiphyte
10. Tree porcupine
11. Bromeliad
12. Red-eyed tree frogs mating and laying eggs
13. Owl butterfly
14. Tent-making bats

• Epiphytes (4) hang from tree trunks and branches. They take nourishment from sunlight and rainwater, not from tree trunks themselves.

• Some tree frogs (12) lay their eggs in pools of water that collect in bromeliads (11).

• Tent-making bats (14) fold leaves in two to make a dry shelter for their young.

• The porcupine (10) has a prehensile tail, which it uses like an extra hand to hold onto twigs and branches.

• Vine snakes (2) are well disguised among the trailing creepers that surround the tree trunks. They hunt lizards and young birds.

THE UNDERSTOREY

*T*he understorey is made up of tall shrubs and trees less than 10 metres tall. The trees of the understorey are usually young trees whose growth has been stunted by the lack of sunshine. They get the chance to grow when one of the "forest giants" comes crashing down, clearing a path in its wake and letting in more light.

In the damp, dim-lit world of the understorey, mosses and algae flourish. They grow on tree trunks, on creepers and even on animals. Some sloths eventually turn dull green, coloured by the algae living on their fur.

But there are patches of brightness among the shadows. Brilliant birds search for insect food among the twining creepers. The glossy green leaves of many understorey creepers are so decorative that they have been cultivated as houseplants.

• The kinkajou's (6) prehensile tail helps it to balance on damp, slippery branches and climb hanging creepers.

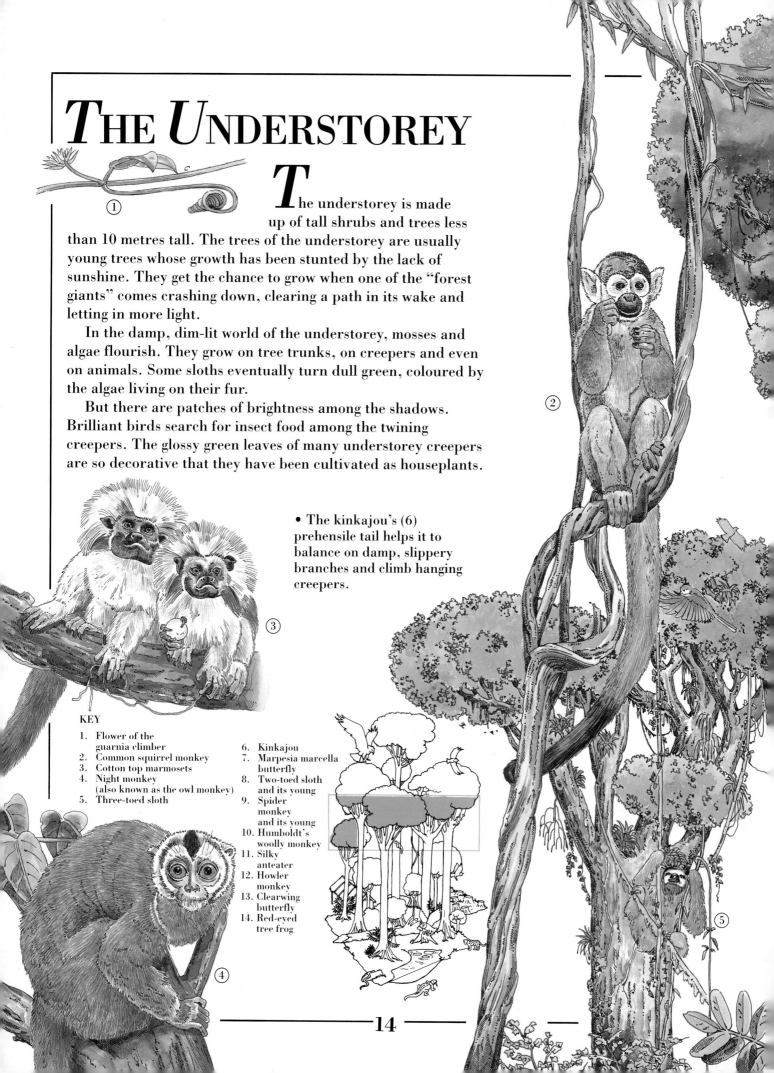

KEY

1. Flower of the guarnia climber
2. Common squirrel monkey
3. Cotton top marmosets
4. Night monkey (also known as the owl monkey)
5. Three-toed sloth
6. Kinkajou
7. Marpesia marcella butterfly
8. Two-toed sloth and its young
9. Spider monkey and its young
10. Humboldt's woolly monkey
11. Silky anteater
12. Howler monkey
13. Clearwing butterfly
14. Red-eyed tree frog

KEY

1. Red squirrel
2. Jaguar
3. Mosses
4. Hummingbird chicks in nest
5. Woolly opossum carrying young on its back
6. Emerald tree boa
7. Blue tanager

⑤

⑥

⑦

IN THE SHADE

*I*n the deep shade of the rain forest, beneath the canopy and the understorey, there is little vegetation. Only mosses and ferns that need little light can survive in this perpetual twilight. However, the shady, damp conditions and the open spaces provide an ideal hunting ground for many large predators.

Jaguars lurk in the bushes or climb the lowest branches to lie in wait for their prey. Their beautiful coats, patterned in splashes of fawn and brown, provide good camouflage in the dappled light.

Great snakes are also skilful hunters. They glide silently along the forest branches to catch roosting birds or to rob their nests. Many snakes are brightly patterned. They have no need of camouflage, and their strong colouring warns off any creature that might dare to attack them.

• Boas (6) do not have chewing teeth, so they swallow their victims whole. To do this, boas dislocate their jawbones if necessary.

• Small, weak animals like the opossum (5) have large eyes and ears to help them detect approaching predators.

EXPLOITATION

①

The rain forests are being cut down for their timber and to make room for ranches, mines and plantations. Every year an area of forest the size of England is destroyed. In 1950, 15 per cent of the world's land area was covered by rain forest. By the year 2000, this figure will be only 7 per cent, if felling continues at the present rate.

The loss of the rain forest has far-reaching consequences. A rain forest acts like a sponge, soaking up the water that falls on it. When the forest is cut down, the rainwater runs away, carrying valuable soil with it. The soil that remains becomes poor in nutrients. The soil that is washed away chokes rivers, which burst their banks in heavy rainfall and can cause extensive flooding. The eroded soil causes further damage when it enters coastal seas and smothers coral reefs.

KEY

1. Golden lion marmoset
2. Roots growing from a tree reach out to cover a fallen tree. Nutrients from decaying trees are passed on to living trees.
3. Roadsides are terraced to prevent banks from collapsing onto the road in the next heavy rainfall.
4. Orange-winged Amazon parrot

② ③

• Forests absorb a great amount of carbon dioxide. When carbon dioxide builds up in the atmosphere it traps the sun's heat, thus warming up the earth's surface. This is known as the "greenhouse effect". Without the rain forests to absorb excess carbon dioxide, the world's climate may change as a result of the greenhouse effect.

④

19

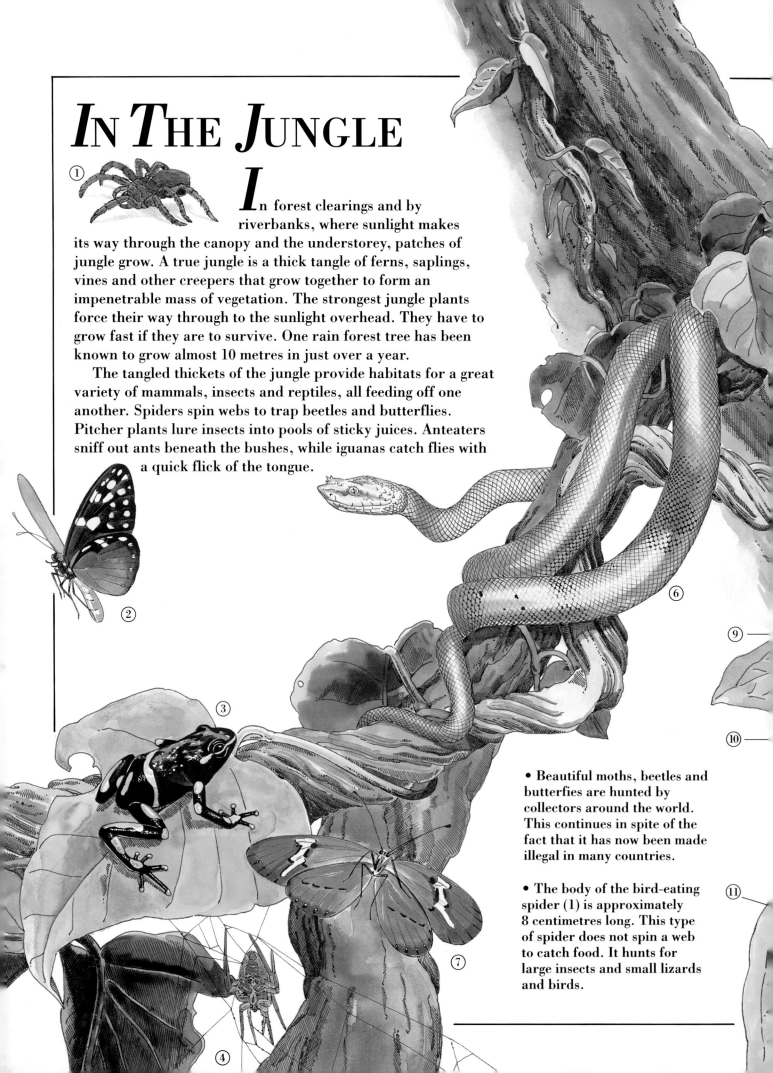

In The Jungle

In forest clearings and by riverbanks, where sunlight makes its way through the canopy and the understorey, patches of jungle grow. A true jungle is a thick tangle of ferns, saplings, vines and other creepers that grow together to form an impenetrable mass of vegetation. The strongest jungle plants force their way through to the sunlight overhead. They have to grow fast if they are to survive. One rain forest tree has been known to grow almost 10 metres in just over a year.

The tangled thickets of the jungle provide habitats for a great variety of mammals, insects and reptiles, all feeding off one another. Spiders spin webs to trap beetles and butterflies. Pitcher plants lure insects into pools of sticky juices. Anteaters sniff out ants beneath the bushes, while iguanas catch flies with a quick flick of the tongue.

• Beautiful moths, beetles and butterfies are hunted by collectors around the world. This continues in spite of the fact that it has now been made illegal in many countries.

• The body of the bird-eating spider (1) is approximately 8 centimetres long. This type of spider does not spin a web to catch food. It hunts for large insects and small lizards and birds.

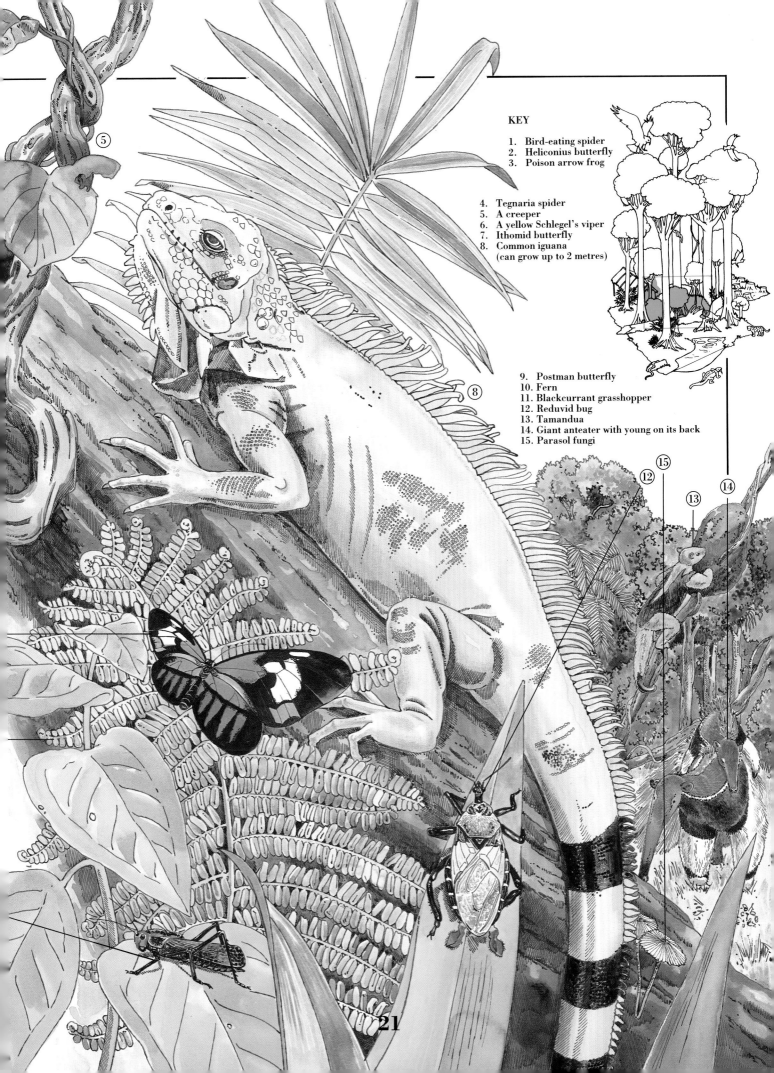

KEY

1. Bird-eating spider
2. Heliconius butterfly
3. Poison arrow frog

4. Tegnaria spider
5. A creeper
6. A yellow Schlegel's viper
7. Ithomid butterfly
8. Common iguana
   (can grow up to 2 metres)

9. Postman butterfly
10. Fern
11. Blackcurrant grasshopper
12. Reduvid bug
13. Tamandua
14. Giant anteater with young on its back
15. Parasol fungi

21

FOREST PEOPLES

②

For centuries, the peoples of the rain forests have lived in harmony with their surroundings. By twentieth-century European standards, their lives seem simple and harsh. In some ways, this is true. But rain forest people have learned how to feed, house, clothe and cure themselves using local products. They have conserved the forest that is their home. They have developed technologies – dugout canoes for transport and blowpipes for hunting – that work effectively and economically. Their cultures are rich in traditional knowledge and beliefs.

But, tragically, old medicines cannot cure new European diseases. Blowpipes are no match for guns or bulldozers. Without money, local people cannot hire lawyers to fight "development". Like their beautiful homeland, today the rain forest peoples are under threat.

• People of the rain forest clear small areas of the forest to build houses and grow crops. After a few years, when the soil becomes exhausted, they move on, and the forest grows again.

KEY

1. Roof thatched with leaves and grasses
2. Timber supports for house roof
3. Hammock beds (traditionally woven from creepers and grasses)
4. Making a dugout boat from a single tree trunk
5. Tree cut for rubber tapping (collecting liquid sap)
6. Blowpipe for hunting
7. Quiver (case for arrows tipped with poison collected from frogs)
8. Facepaint and beads made from forest earth, plants and seeds

THE FOREST FLOOR

①

Rain forest soils are poor, thin and stony. Any goodness they contain comes from the mass of rotting debris that covers the forest floor. In one year, over 10 tonnes of litter rains down on a single hectare of forest floor. The forest litter, fallen tree trunks and the remains of dead creatures all decay rapidly in the damp warmth, largely through the action of fungi, termites and other organisms, creating a layer of humus.

The forest floor forms an ideal environment for many types of creatures. Ants and termites make nests and "castles" in the crumbly soil. The fallen leaves and rotting wood are home to reptiles and thousands of insects and other creepy-crawlies. Shy deer, and other mammals that cannot climb, feed on the shrubs, herbs and grasses that grow in open spaces between tall trees.

KEY

1. Millipede
2. Flaming poison arrow frog sitting on a fungus
3. Pit viper
4. Litter frog
5. Fallen tree trunk
6. Coatimundi and young
7. White tailed deer
8. Cock of the rock
9. Ocelot
10. Slender lizard
11. Nightjar

• Poison arrow frogs produce venom in glands beneath the skin. The poison from one species – the golden arrow frog – is the most deadly ever discovered.

• Venom from a pit viper (3) can also kill. It bites using remarkable fangs that fold away when not in use.

③

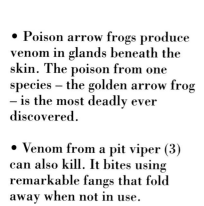

②

④

• Nightjars (11) are unusual because they feed at night on insects. They have huge eyes for seeing in the dark.

①

②

③

④

⑤

⑥

⑦

• Capybara (4) are close relatives of our pet guinea pigs, but much larger. They can grow 1.3 metres tall.

• A baby hoatzin (16) uses the claws on its wings to cling to branches. It drops into the water below to escape its enemies.

• Sadly, giant otters (12) are becoming increasingly rare because they are hunted for their thick, glossy fur.

THE RIVERBANK

*T*he roots and fresh green shoots of many rain forest plants form clumps and thickets, lining the riverbank. This damp, warm, sunny layer of the forest is home to many reptiles and amphibians. Snakes, frogs, toads and terrapins bask in the sunshine, then plunge into the cool waters in search of food.

Other riverbank creatures, such as alligators and otters, are keen hunters; they live mostly on fish. Wading birds search for insects in the shallows, keeping watch for alligators and snakes. Terrapins scavenge along the river bottom. Seeds from creepers, bushes and trees germinate in the riverbank soil, ready to begin a new generation of rain forest life.

KEY

1. Giant armadillo
2. Anaconda
3. Hoatzin
4. Capybara with its young
5. Alligator
6. Buttress roots
7. Limpkin
8. Roseate spoonbills
9. Scarlet ibis
10. Baird's tapir
11. Water lilies
12. Giant otters
13. Basilisk lizard
14. Terrapins
15. Electric eel
16. Baby hoatzin

UNDERWATER

*T*he swirling river waters form the lowest level of habitation for rain forest life. The mighty Amazon River flows over 6400 kilometres, from the snowy Andes mountains to the sea. It is so deep that ocean-going liners can sail upstream for more than half its length. At the estuary, it measures 320 kilometres across.

Over 1500 species of fish, from tiny, brilliantly coloured tetras to huge, sinister stingrays, live in the rain forest rivers. Piranha fish eat animals that fall into the river. Elegant angel fish glide among the reeds. One of the few species of freshwater dolphins swims in the Amazon River and its streams. Insects lay eggs on the water's surface, and newly hatched tadpoles drop from huge forest leaves to join the teeming river life.

KEY

1. Piranha fish
2. Freshwater dolphins
3. Electric eel
4. Terrapin
5. Hatchet fish
6. Silver dollar
7. Cardinal tetra
8. Neon tetras
9. Chocolate cichlid
10. Mata-mata turtle
11. Stingray
12. Discus fish
13. Rosy tetra
14. Swordtail
15. Hidden necked turtle and its young
16. Serpa tetra
17. Freshwater angel fish
18. Striped anostomus
19. Dwarf pencil fish
20. Spotted head-stander
21. Anaconda
22. Cayman
23. Damselfly
24. Tree frog tadpoles still in their jelly

• The male chocolate cichlid (9) protects its young from predators by hiding them in its mouth.

• Stingrays (11) lurk on the river bed. They are dull-coloured, so they can lie hidden among mud and stones. Spines on their tails act as protection from enemies.

• Some rain forest frogs lay their eggs in pools of water trapped in the leaves. This saves the eggs from being eaten by fish.

• Anaconda snakes (21) are among the largest creatures of the rain forest. They can grow up to 9 metres long.

• The head of the mata-mata turtle (10) is covered with waving flaps of skin, to make it look bigger and more impressive.

29

GLOSSARY

Algae
Very simple plants that can consist of one cell or chains or sheets of cells and live in water or on damp surfaces.

Amphibian
A back-boned creature with soft, moist skin that can survive in water and on land. Their young hatch from jelly-like eggs. Newts, salamanders, frogs and toads are amphibians.

Blowpipe
A hollowed-out stick, used in hunting by rain forest peoples. Hunters blow down the pipe to shoot the dart forward.

Bromeliad
A plant of the pineapple family, usually with stiff, leathery leaves that form a rosette.

Buttress roots
Wing-like growths that spread out from the trunk of a rain forest tree down to the ground to act as supports.

Camouflage
Colour or shape that blends in with the surroundings.

Canopy
The thick layer of vegetation that forms the "roof" of the rain forest, about 30–40 metres above the ground.

Dugout canoe
A boat made from a single hollowed-out tree trunk. The wood is chopped out with axes or burned away by fire.

Environment
The surrounding conditions that occur in the places where plants, animals or people live.

Epiphyte
A plant that grows on another plant but not as a parasite. Epiphytes get water from raindrops trapped in their leaves, and not through their roots as other plants do. Also known as air plants.

Fertile
(Used to describe soils.) Full of the food and nourishment that help plants grow.

Forest giants
The tallest trees in the forest.

Fungi
Plant-like organisms that cannot make their own food as most plants do. Fungi are either parasites on living organisms or they feed on dead organic material. Mushrooms are an example of a fungus.

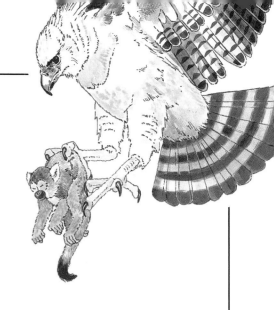

Gland
A part of the body.
Mammals, reptiles and
insects all have glands.
Glands produce various
chemicals essential to life
and health. Some of
these chemicals act as
"messengers" within the
body; others, such as the
poison produced by some
frogs, help protect creatures
from attack.

Humus
Loose, soft soil that is made
up of decayed plant and
animal matter.

Jungle
A thick tangle of vegetation.
Rain forests have patches of
jungle, but they are usually
more open.

Litter
Dead leaves, seeds, flowers,
twigs and other material
that gather on the forest
floor and form part of the
soil.

Mammals
Warm-blooded animals that
are usually covered with
hair or fur and feed their
young on milk.

Parasites
Plants or animals that rely
on "host" species for food to
stay alive. Parasitic plants
and animals
weaken the host,
but rarely kill it.
If they did, the parasites
would die themselves.

Plantation
Specially cleared land
where plants, for example,
banana and rubber trees,
are cultivated for human
use. Carefully managed
plantations need not
damage the rain forest.
Badly run plantations can
destroy it for ever.

Predator
An animal that hunts and
eats another animal.

Prehensile
Capable of grasping things.

Prey
An animal that is hunted
and killed by other animals
for food.

Ranch
A large farm where huge
numbers of cattle are
usually left free to roam
over wide open spaces.
Cattle ranchers have cut
down vast areas of rain
forest to provide room for
their cattle to roam.
This has caused serious
damage to the forests in
South America.

Reptiles
Cold-blooded, back-boned
animals with scaly skin
whose young are produced
in waterproof eggs.
Alligators, snakes and
turtles are reptiles.

Roosting
Settling in a safe place
to sleep.

Sapling
A young tree.

Scavenge
To search for leftover food
among litter and the
remains of dead creatures.

Species
A distinct group of animals
or plants that is different
from all other groups.
Individuals of the same
species can interbreed.

Spore
A single-celled unit from
which a new fungus can
grow.

Understorey
The area of the rain forest
beneath the canopy and
above the ground.

Venom
Poison. Often snake poison.

Vine
A plant with a long stem
that grows along the ground
or clings to tree trunks.

INDEX

References in bold type refer to illustrations.

algae 14, 30
alligators **26**, 27, **29**
Amazon River 28
amphibians 27, 30
anacondas **26**, 29, **29**
Andes mountains 28
angel fish 28, **29**
anteaters **10**, 15, 18, **19**
ants 12, **12**, 18, 20
armadillos **26**

bats 12, 13, **13**
beetles 18
birds **8-9**, 10, **10**, 11, 13, 14, 17, 18, **21**, 27, **27**, **29**
blowpipes 22, **23**, 30
boas 17, **17**
bromeliads **9**, **11**, 12, 13, **13**, 30
butterflies **10**, **11**, 12, 13, **13**, **15**, 18, **18-19**
buttress roots 9, **24**, **27**, 30

camouflage 12, 17, 30
canopy 6, 9, **10-11**, 17, 30
capybaras 26, **26**
chocolate cichlids 28, **28**
climate 24
creepers 6, 13, 14, 18, **19**, 27

deer 20, **21**
destruction of rain forests 24-5
dolphins 28, **28**
dugout canoes 22, **23**, 30

electric eels **27**, 28
emergent layer 6, 8-9
epiphytes **12**, 13, 30

ferns 6, 12, **12**, 17, 18, **19**
fish 28, **28-9**
forest floor 6, 9, 10, 12, 20-21
forest giants 6, 8, 9, 14, 30
frogs **11**, 12, 13, **13**, **15**, **18**, 20, **20**, 27, 29
fungi 6, 12, **19**, 20, 30

greenhouse effect 24

harpy eagles 10, **10**
hoatzins 26, **26**, 27
houses 22, **22-3**
hummingbirds **9**, 10, **10**, 16
hunting 17, 19

iguanas **11**, **12**, 18, **19**
insects 6, **12**, 18, **18-19**, 20, 28

jackamars **8**
jacobin monkeys **9**
jaguars **16**, 17
jungle 6, 18-19, 31

kinkajous 14, **14**

litter 6, 20, 31
lizards 12, 13, 18, **21**, 27

macaws **9**
mammals 10, 12, 18, 20, 30
marmosets 14, **24**
millipedes **20**
monkeys 9, 10, **10-11**, **14-15**
mosses 6, 12, **12-13**, 14, **16**, 17
moths 12, 18

nightjars 21, **21**
night monkeys 14

ocelots **21**
opossums 17, **17**
orchids 10, 12
otters 26, 27, **27**

parasites 20, 31
parrots **11**, 25
people of the rain forest **22-3**
piranha fish 28, **28**
pitcher plants **18**
plantations 24, 31
porcupines 13, **13**
praying mantis **10**
predators 17, 28, 31

quetzals **8**

rainfall 10
red-faced ukaris **10**
reptiles 12, 18, 20, 27, 31
riverbanks 6, 18, 26-7

scarlet ibis **27**
sloths 10, 11, **11**, 14, **15**
snakes **11**, 12, **12**, 13, 17, **17**, 18, 20, **20**, **26**, 27, 29, **29**
spider monkeys **9**, 15
spiders 18, **18**
spoonbills 27
squirrel monkeys **9**, 10, 14
squirrels **16**
stingrays 28, **29**

tadpoles 28, **29**
tanagers 10, 17
tapirs **26**
termites 20
terrapins 27, **27**, 28
tetras 28, **28**
timber 24
toads 27
toucans 9, 10
trees 8, 9, 12, 14, 16, 18, **23**, 24, 27
turtles 29, **29**

understorey 6, **14-15**, 17, 18, 31

vines 18, 31
vultures 8, **8**

wasps 12, **12**
woolly monkeys **11**, 15